Angels Walk Among Us

"To bring unstoppable hope
From the Lord
of the Impossible"

*Psalm 91:11-12 "I the Lord will command My angels concerning you.
To guard you in all your ways, they will pick you up in their hands..."*

Introduction

I am 66 years old and I have come to believe that this life we all live, is a journey. As we walk through it there are many things that happen that have no reasonable rational explanation. These events become our memories. Our memories when we pass them on to others become our story. We all have a story.

It is my belief that if we will pass our stories on to others with integrity and a humble heart, those stories can make a difference in the lives of the hearers.

It is with those core values that I will attempt to tell my story. My goal is that you the reader will find hope in the random acts of kindness that were shown to me, as a vital part of my journey. It doesn't matter whether they were done to or for myself or whether they were done to or for others I may have encountered along my journey. To the best of my ability I will recount my memories as true and accurate as possible.

Well here goes. I will give my best effort to present the facts, and just tell the truth. Thank you for this opportunity to tell my story!

These are my stories

Story #1

Something Supernatural

When I was about 11 or 12 years old an apartment building was being built right over the back fence of the home my family was living in. Three of my friends and me were over at the construction site playing and we went down into the hole that had been dug to construct the pool for the apartments. We all decided to try to dig a tunnel into the side walls of what would be the pool. We were having a competition to see who could dig one big enough to crawl all the way into the tunnel we were digging. It was getting late, so we decided to come back and finish the next day. It was summer break and we were not in school.

After dinner that night I snuck back over to dig some more so that in the morning when we all met there to dig again, I would be sure to win. It started to get dark, so I quit and went home. In the morning when my friends got there we went back over to finish our tunnels and see who would win the competition. In less than a minute my tunnel caved in with me laying inside it. I couldn't move or breathe; my feet were the only things sticking out. My friends came over and began to dig around me and try to pull me out. I'm sure it took them several minutes to get me out. I had sandy soil up in my nose, in my eyes, and my ears were full of dirt!

I don't know why I didn't suffocate buried in the dirt while my friends were trying to dig me out. But the greater mystery to me was why the tunnel I was digging in didn't cave in on me the night before when I was there digging by myself. Had the dirt gave way then I would have been found dead there the next morning with just my feel sticking out of the dirt. That was my first memory of something supernatural at work in my life.

Story #2

I decided to trust

I was a troubled child and had been in trouble a few times before I got out of Junior High. I had been suspended a couple of times for fighting and other behavior problems. I was in eighth grade and I was 13 years old. I had decided I didn't want to live anymore. After school walking home I had to pass a field that had the large electrical towers with the electrical wires fastened to the top of them. I had decided I was going to climb to the top of the towers and grab on to the electrical wires while sitting on the steel cross beam.

The towers were about 80 feet tall where I could reach out and grab the wires. So, I began climbing up the tower. It took several minutes to get to the top. As I turned around to sit down at the top, a police car had entered the field and was only about 100 feet from me. One of the officers knew my name and began to talk to me with patience and kindness. They were right underneath me now and he got out of his car and continued to talk to me this time without the microphone. I asked him if I was in trouble and if he was going to take me to jail. He said no. They just wanted to get me down safely. I told him I could climb back down if he would promise I wasn't in trouble. He asked me if I was hungry and told me they would take me to the A&W Root Beer Burger place about a block away if I would just come down.

I thought he might be lying but I decided to trust him and came down. A few minutes later on I was on the ground. He asked me what I was doing up there, so I told him the truth that "I just didn't want to live anymore."

He and his partner took me to the A&W and got me something to eat and talked to me for an hour or so. He knew where I lived and told me they were going to take me home. It was less than a mile to my home. They both gave me their phone numbers and told me if I ever felt that way again that I could call either one of them and we would go back to the A&W and talk about it. In less than a minute I would have been dead had God not sent these two men into that field with calm gentle spirits. Because of how they spoke to me and treated me gave birth to a seed of hope that began to grow in me from that day. I didn't consider taking my own life again for over 20 years. The second and last time I considered ending my life is another story that will be told later in this book.

Story #3

God showed up

It was Christmas time and I was 14 years old. One of our neighbors had a cabin in the mountains about 70 miles from our home and they told my parents that we could use it for the holiday. We went up there and it was snowing heavily the night we went. My dad dropped us off and had to go back home and was going to come back up in the morning. He had not returned by mid-day, so my mom asked my brother and I to go to the ranger station about two miles away to use their phone to call home and see if he was okay and if he was coming back up.

We went to the main highway and decided to hitch hike to the Ranger Station instead of walking in the snow. A small pickup truck stopped with two men and a woman in the cab. There was a shell on the back, and they told us to get in the back and they would drop us at the Ranger station. We started up the road and we could see out the windows of the shell of the truck. We came to the Ranger Station and the driver kept going. We banged on the back window of the cab of the truck to stop and let us out of the truck; they laughed at us and went faster. I was frightened and didn't know what to do. There were skis and poles and stuff in the back of the truck where we were, and the window of the shell was not latched. My brother and I decided to start throwing the skis and gear out of the back of the truck and when they stopped to retrieve it, we would jump out and run.

They just laughed harder and went faster. We decided we were going to jump out of the truck. My brother was a year older and much bigger than me, so he decided to go first. We let down the tail gate and he climbed to the end of it. The truck came to a sharp curve and had to slow down at the curve. My brother let go and dropped to the street. They stepped on the gas and there was a long straight section of road. My brother was telling me to get out. I got into position and lowered my feet. The truck was going about 30 miles an hour by this time. When my toes touched the street, I was jerked out of the truck and my forehead hit the tail gate and then I went down hard and my forehead slammed into the street.

9

The impact and speed caused me to roll over the snow berm and down the hillside a few feet. I was knocked out for a moment or two. When I opened my eyes, I could see a marker pole a few feet above me. I climbed up the snowbank and grabbed the pole and climbed over to the street side and climbed down to the highway. My brother was walking towards me. I made sure to remember the number on the pole so I could tell the Rangers where this all happened.

My brother told me there were two large knots on my forehead (later I found out I had a concussion). We went back to the Ranger Station and told them what happened. I told them the mile post marker I climbed out on and they looked puzzled. They asked if I was sure that was the number and I said yes. They said that it wasn't possible. Where that marker is, is a sheer drop for 100 feet to the bottom of the canyon.

The Rangers decided to drive me back there to prove to me I was wrong. From the time we left that place and went to the Ranger Station and got back again there had been an avalanche there at that place. When we looked over the side all the snow there had fallen down into the canyon. There was a three feet wide and six feet long drainpipe sticking out from under the road and on top of that pipe was my body imprint into the little bit of snow that was left on the top of it and the footprints coming from there up to the mile posts marker. Everything on both sides of it were gone, they had dropped into the canyon. Had I gone over that berm anywhere but the exact place I did, I would have gone 100 feet down into the canyon. I know God showed up in one form or another to save my life that day.

The people who had been in the cab of the truck were arrested later that day. They were high on drugs and had stolen the truck. The ski gear we had been throwing out into the highway didn't even belong to them. By the time we returned to the cabin, my dad was there.

Story #4

Jesus Loves Me

At the end of my sophomore year of high school, I started going to Church on Monday and Friday nights with a group of kids. I was fifteen at the time. On the Friday night of Memorial

Weekend of 1970, we got there a little later than usual because of traffic and church hadn't started yet but it was full, so, we stood outside in the planter. The church had large glass windows so we could still see and there were speakers outside so we could hear. I don't remember what the pastor talked about. I wasn't a believer at that time; I guess you could say I was a "seeker." But I will never forget what happened at the end. About 20 minutes before the pastor finished talking it started to rain. Lightly at first, but it was raining hard when it ended. I was standing there, soaking wet, looking through the glass at the pastor and when he finished teaching he stood up and looked out the window in my direction and he pointed that way and said, "Jesus is here tonight to tell you He loves you.", I began to look around and he said, "No you, and I put my hands on my chest and he said, "Yes, you. He wants you know He loves you deeply." At that moment I was overwhelmed with the presence of God for the first time in my life. I fell to the mud and began to weep. After crying for some time my friends helped me up and took me inside. I was all muddy and soaking wet. The Pastor came up and hugged me and gave me a New Testament Bible with the Psalms in the back of it. I didn't own a Bible. In fact,

Truth be told, I had never read a whole book of any kind, but I spent that whole weekend reading that book and by Monday afternoon I had finished the New Testament and the Psalms.

I met Jesus that night and became a part of His family. Until that night in May of 1970, (I was going to be sixteen years old in two months from that very day), I could not remember any one ever telling me that they loved me. Not Parents, Grand Parents, family, friends, no one, not once, ever. Jesus, the maker and creator of everything, the King of All "sought me out and found me and drew me to Himself specifically to tell me that "He loved me deeply." This moment in time left me undone for the next 50 years.

Through the ups, downs, good, and bad, (and I experienced some of each as you will see in the rest of my stories). He remained faithful, and He loves you all the same and always has!

Story #5

It Just Wasn't Possible

I was 16 and my brother and I played softball on a team with my dad and our uncle. We had gone to play a game and shortly after the game started; it began to rain so they called the game. I was riding in a car with my brother, he was driving the car. We approached a traffic light that had just turned yellow and that is where we needed to turn. He stepped on the gas and began the turn. Due to the wet road conditions the car began to slide on the road. Because it was a left turn we were making, it was the passenger side of the car that was sliding towards the curb. As we were about to hit the curb I looked up and saw a concrete bus bench right in front of the car. I don't remember the next few seconds; all I remember was the sound of glass breaking. When I opened my eyes, it was dark all around me and I was in a pile of broken glass wadded up under the dashboard of the car. I couldn't get out. My brother reached in from the driver's side and took my hand and helped pull me out under the steering wheel.

Where the car had jumped the curb there was a steel guide wire supporting a telephone pole. That steel cable had slammed into my side of the car and broke both the side windows then the front of the car hit the bus bench. When it did, the concrete side support snapped off and came through the front windshield shattering the window and came through the front seat where I had been sitting and landed in the back seat. This all happened so fast I didn't have time to even think of what I should do. I did not put myself under the glove box in that little tiny space. In fact, it wasn't even possible. We had the car towed home. After my dad cleaned all the glass out of it, he tried to help me crawl into that space and we tried three times and I couldn't fit in there. Yet somehow in a moment of time before impact that is where I was placed.

The steel cable would have hit me in the neck; the concrete that came through the window with such force would have hit me right in the face. Either of them could have killed me. Somehow in a second of time God or one of His angels wadded me up and tucked me into the only place I would be safe from harm. Thank you, Jesus!!!

Story #6

Supernatural Protection

I was 17 when four of my friends and I were going to my Grandma's ranch. We were in a car with a full trunk. This was in 1972 and the car was an early 60's model. This was before seat belts were required so none of us had them on. We were carrying two five-gallon cans full of gas for the tractor. We also were carrying several rifles and handguns to do some target shooting with 1,000 rounds of ammunition.

We had to go several miles down a curvy country road once we got off the main highway. My friend was driving, and another was riding shot gun. The other three of us were in the back seat. As we came around a sharp left curve, we went a little off the road into the soft gravel. When we came back onto the road with the back tires it turned the car sideways and the car flipped over. The car flipped up and rolled over again. Before it was done it flipped over five times and ended up on its side with the passenger side to the top. We began to talk to each other to see if everyone was okay. Then we all climbed out the windows that were facing up. When we all got out of the car, we thought we could push it over to be upright on the tires. So, we did. None of the tires were flat. We opened the trunk, and everything was still in it and not broken. The roof was smashed down and all the windows were broken out of it.

The driver of the car was the only one hurt, he had a small cut on his left arm when the car skidded to a stop right on his door. We wanted to see if it would start and it did, so we drove the 45 miles home in it just as it was. The possibilities of what could have happened that day are endless. The lives that could have been lost, the bones that could have been broken, the fires that could have started, yet one or more of God's angels showed up and five young men walked away grateful.

Story #7

Grace in The Little Things

When I was 17 after graduating high school, I went to church camp that summer. I drove my pickup truck there after work on a Friday night. I was only going to stay the weekend. I had to be back at work the following Monday and the camp was about 80 miles from my home.

When it was time to leave summer camp and I was to go home, I knew I needed to put gas in the truck. So I left camp and headed down the mountain. As I came down off the mountain, just before I got to the freeway, I stopped at a service station and reached under the seat to get out my wallet, which is where I normally kept it. However, it wasn't there. I prayed, asking God to please tell me where I had put my wallet. I believe God spoke to my heart and told me my wallet was in the pocket of my work pants that I had left behind. So, I prayed again that God would make the gas last so that I could make it home. I had about 45 more miles to go to get home and my gas gauge was extremely close to empty. Yet I had peace in my heart that I should continue driving home and that I would make it.

As soon as I got on the freeway my tank read empty. The truck began to sputter, and I would pray "O Sweet Jesus get me home. Please get me home." Then the sputtering began again about 10 miles further down the road. I would pray that same prayer again and the sputtering would stop for about 10 more miles. This went on all the way home. I pulled into the driveway, left the engine running, ran to my bedroom and there was my wallet, in my work pants! I grabbed it and went around the corner to the gas station. As soon as I started to go up the driveway of the gas station, the motor stopped. I was out of gas. I coasted to the pump. I got my money out with a smile. As I pumped the gas, God reminded me the teaching at the camp that weekend was "My God is able to do exceedingly abundantly above all we ask or think." In my prayers all the way home I continued to ask, "Just get me home, and please get me home." I didn't even consider that I would need to go further than home and that I would need to get back to the gas station before I ran out of gas. But my sweet Jesus went beyond what I asked, because He knew. He had done exceedingly abundantly above all I had asked for!

Story #8

He Leads, Even in the Darkness

I was almost 19 and my church was taking a group to Hawaii to share some hope and love to the Marine Bases over there and I decided to go. On one of the islands where we were there was an active volcano. The pastor made arrangements for us to take a bus ride to where we could walk out on the lava that had cooled. Not too far from where it was still flowing. It was amazing. It was dark and all the ground around us was black. After walking for about 20 minutes, we started back towards the bus. I felt in my spirit we were going the wrong way. Yet the pastor was peaceful and didn't agree. He believed they were heading correctly. So, I told him I was going to go a different way. He said that when I got back to the road just walk up and I would then find the bus and they would wait for me.

So, I went where the peace of my spirit was leading me. In about a half an hour I came over a small hill and about 100 yards in front of me was the bus. I came off the slope and right into the door of the bus. I got comfortable and went to sleep. About two hours later the pastor got there with the rest of the group. They had come out on the road about four miles from the bus. He stepped onto the bus and he asked the driver if I was there and he told him I had been sleeping for a couple of hours. The pastor walked up to me with a big smile on his face and put his hand on my shoulder. I felt his love and respect without him needing to speak a single word. The Fathers leading hadn't failed me.

Story #9

Uncommon Mercy

I was 19 years old and two friends and I were in the drive thru of a fast food place. There was a couple of cars in front of me, one at the window and another directly in front of me. The car in front of me had four young men in it; the car in front of them only had the driver in it. All of a sudden, the car in front of me intentionally bumps into the car in front of it. Then the driver of the car backed up and did it again with more force than the first time. After the second time, the driver of the front car got out to see the damage that may have occurred. When he got to the back of his car all four of the young men got out of their car. They began to push and slap the man whose car they had rammed.

I told my friend to drive my car and I got out to stop them. As I ran towards them, the man that was being abused started to run away towards the street in front of us. Two of the men began to chase him. I was about to overtake them when the man ran out into the street and was hit by a big semi-truck. He flew into the air and landed headfirst in the street. The two men chasing him ran back to their car and pushed his car out of their way and drove off. I went to the man that was lying in the street. The truck driver got out of his rig. I told him to call 911.

It had been raining lightly for a while. I got on my knees and leaned over the man, he wasn't breathing, and I checked his pulse and he had none. I had recently received a spiritual gift called "speaking in other tongues." It is a way of prayer that doesn't go through our intellect but comes straight from our spirits to the heart of God. I began to pray over the man while trying to shield his face from the rain. I stayed there in the street with him until the police and paramedics got there. The police wanted me to tell them what had happened, and I told them what I saw. One of my friends who had moved my car out of the drive thru and stayed in it while this was going on had written down the license plate number of the car with the men in it. The police took my phone number and said they may call me to be a witness at court.

I got the call and was asked to be in court. I showed up at court and in the back of the court room I saw a man who looked like the man who had been killed by the truck. He was sitting with two people who looked like they could be his parents. The judge called the case number and I went forward as a witness. The Judge said they caught the men and they had pleaded guilty and were in jail and I was dismissed.

As I got to the back of the court room the man I had noticed earlier, who I had thought dead, followed me into the hallway and stopped me. The man asked me if I was the one who had prayed for him. I told them I was. He asked me where I'd learned to speak Portuguese and I told him I don't. He shared that while I was praying over him, he heard me praying for him in his native language. He'd felt that he was in heaven and that he'd heard me calling him back for his unborn children and the woman he was pledged to marry. That it wasn't his time and that those men had attempted to steal what wasn't rightly theirs to take. That our Heavenly Father was going to make it right. I told him I had no idea what I was praying, I was just allowing my spirit to pray and that my spirit was crying out to God's Spirit. He told me he had died and that on the way to the hospital they revived him, and he came back to life. And those prayers that God was calling out were what gave him the strength and courage to fight to live. The people with him were his parents and he was an only child and was about to be married, and how excited they were to become Grandparents. We all hugged and gave God the glory. Only our God has the power and compassion to make something like this occur.

Story #10

Angels All Around

When I was 22 years old I had just moved to Oregon and a woman was coming to speak at a town about 100 miles from where I had moved. I had planned to leave early and go to hear her speak. I was with three other people and my dog (a full-grown Black Lab). I was driving a small station wagon. There were two ways to get to the town we were going to. One was straight down the highway; the other was up over the mountain pass then down the backside. They both take about the same time, so I chose to go over the mountain pass (the weather was supposed to be good).

About halfway up the mountain, a light rain started. I knew we would be up and over the pass in about 20 minutes. We were about three miles to the summit when the rain turned to snow. It wasn't snowing hard, so I continued to press forward. We just cleared the summit and there was about a mile of straight highway, and then I would be heading down the other side and all would be good.

There was a layer of wet snow across the road. I had never driven in the snow before. All of a sudden, I was hydroplaning. I had no control of my steering wheel at all. I took my foot off the gas. I began to drift towards the middle of the road. Soon I crossed the center divider. Coming right at me was a Continental Trail Ways bus. I knew he couldn't do anything either or he could lose control of his bus. As I floated in front of him on the wrong side of the highway, I moved to his left into the next oncoming traffic lane. We were so close I felt my car move from the wind of the bus as it went by me at about 40 miles an hour. Just as I cleared the bus, I saw a four by four truck coming right towards me. Since the bus had been so big I had no idea that he was coming up the road and I was floating across the road in front of him. He couldn't use his break either or risk losing control. He must have taken his foot off the gas; as he had been accelerating to pass the bus. He squeezed over behind the bus. Again, so close that I could again feel the car move as the wind went by my car.

I was out of traffic lanes now, on the shoulder still heading the wrong way on a four-lane mountain highway in the snow. I still had no control of the car; and I just knew it was going to go off the road on the wrong side of the highway. As the front of the car went off the road it sank down in pea gravel that was about two feet deep. It caused the car to stop just in front of a large Pine Tree. The tree was about three feet across at the trunk. I got out went to the front of the car. It was just touching the tree, but not enough to have even knocked the bark off.

We called for a tow truck and were back on the road in half of an hour. The snow had stopped and within 10 minutes we were below snow LINE? I drove to the place where the speaker was and got there 10 minutes before it started. Again, this potential tragedy was avoided by the grace, mercy, and goodness of a compassionate God, no other reason. Not chance, not luck, not fate. God and God alone!

Story #11

Why Me Lord?

I was working as a roofer in Oregon and was about 24. We were doing a large commercial building. We were running two kettles on the ground to pump up enough hot tar up to the roof. We were using a low melt tar called pitch. When this material gets too hot, it will give off a green smoke and it is very potent and will burn your nose when you breathe it in. Up on the roof it was my job to fill a container called a low boy from the pump by pulling a cord, so as to get the hot tar to what is called a spreader. When I did this, there was green smoke everywhere. So I brought this to the foreman and told me to go to the ground and find out why the tar was so hot.

I went to the ground and the man that was filling the kettle with the 100-pound kegs of tar was gone. I couldn't find him anywhere. So, I looked at the thermometer on the kettle and it was at 400 degrees and way hotter than what it should be. So, I opened the kettle which was way hotter than it should be. It was about to ignite. So I broke up some small pieces of hardened tar to cool off what was in the kettle. Small pieces melt faster so they cool the tar down. Then I started to lower a full 100-pound keg in to fill the kettle. When I started to lower it in, two-thirds of it broke off and splashed into the kettle sending a large wave of hot tar to the back of the kettle. When it had hit the back wall of the kettle it came forward larger and with more force than it went back. This all happened in a couple of seconds. I just closed my eyes and waited for the hot tar to splash up in my face and burn my face off.

In a couple of seconds when I didn't feel the pain of my flesh burning I opened my eyes and looked down and around and I could see some of the tar on the toes of my boots and as I looked beside and behind me, there was tar all over the ground even 12 feet behind me. As I looked at the splash pattern on the ground it had spread out as though I was five feet wide and 10 feet tall in the outline of an angel. I got on my knees right there and wept thanking God for His goodness in sending His angel to protect me.

Just then, the man that was supposed to be filling the kettle walked up. He had been in the outhouse, sick and unable to get back to his job.

It sometimes is not our faith, but His faithfulness. At my moment of crisis, I didn't even have one second to pray. Yet He came anyway because of my need of Him.

Story #12

Pray Harder

I was 26 years old. I had gone in for surgery to have my left wrist fused. I had gone through two previous surgeries trying to repair that wrist and they were unsuccessful. After the surgery I went home. The next day I was having chest pain and trouble breathing. So, I went back to the hospital to the Emergency Room. They admitted me and ran some test.

I had pneumonia in my right lung due to an infection I had picked up while in the hospital. After two days I began having trouble with my left lung and it had gotten the infection also. Now I was dealing with double pneumonia. After a couple of days, both lungs were barely functioning.

The sun had just gone down and I was struggling just to breathe at all. The doctor came and told me if my condition didn't change in the next 20 minutes, he was going to open me up and put me on an iron lung.

I hit the nurse button and asked for a phone (choking out the words). Her response was "You can't even talk, why do you want a phone?" I replied, "PHONE NOW"!! In a couple of minutes, they had a phone hooked up at my bed. I called home and my wife answered. (We had a three-year-old and a newborn at home). When she answered the phone all I could say was "Pray." She responded through tears, "We are all praying." I said, "Pray harder." Then hung up the phone and now I was angry, angry at God, why He would let this happen. I had the responsibility of this family He had given me. Now I'm about to die and leave them. I was not happy and didn't even want to talk to God. However, I had known Him and walked life out with Him for over 10 years now and I had experienced His presence showing up many times for many reasons and change the outcome of the reality I was living in.

So, I closed my eyes to pray. Still angry, still frustrated, and still in tremendous pain I said, "Why have you done this, where are you? Why would You give me this responsibility only to take me away and abandon the family that You have given me?" Then God spoke to my heart. I knew that still small voice, I knew it well. He had spoken to me many times over the past 10 years and the only word He spoke to me was "SING."

I responded (in my mind. I could no longer speak words out of my mouth). "What do You mean sing? I can't sing. I can't even talk." And the word came back to me again a second time, "SING." At that moment a peace came over me and I was no longer angry at a distant King that I served, I was broken as I lay in the presence of my Loving Father! So, I asked in my thoughts "What do you want me to sing?" A few seconds went by. Then He spoke again, "More love, more power, more of you in my life." I was familiar with this worship song.

So, in my thoughts I began to sing "More love, more power, more of You in my life." God spoke and I sensed that He was asking for all of me – whatever it looked like or sounded like, no matter how weak or broken I was, He would accept no less than all of me!

So, I started to try to speak the words through coughing and choking, very faintly the words came out. When I finished, God spoke again. He said, "AGAIN." I struggled through the words one more time. He spoke again, this time all God said was "louder." This time I was going to sing as loud as I could if it was the last breath I took. (He was going to get all of me).

This time I didn't cough, or choke and the words came out clear, "more love, more power, more of You in my life." Although it was very faint, and there was still a great deal of pain in my chest. Again, God said "LOUDER." I tried to breath deeper so I could sing louder and

then I sang "More love, more power, more of You in my life" again and sang out "More love,

more power, more of You in my life." This time it came out with the volume of a normal talking voice, however my pain level dropped in half. So, I breathed in deep again and sang out "More love, more power, more of You in my life." This time it was a normal singing volume and I had no more pain in my chest.

I sang the lines to the song over and over again until the nurses at the end of the hall came in and told me I had to be quiet. I was making too much noise.

From the time I called my wife for prayer to the time the nurses came to ask me to be quiet was just about 20 minutes. The doctor came back in expecting to send me to surgery and instead he found me totally healed. Both lungs were fully inflated with no pain. He told me he wanted me to spend the night and keep me on IV's just to be sure.

I called by wife back. By this time, it had been an hour from when she got my desperate call. I told her God had showed up and healed me and she could come pick me up in the morning. This time she was crying with tears of joy rather than pain.

Story #13

Unstoppable Hope

I was 27 years old and lived in a small mountain community. There was one hospital and a half a dozen churches. For the church I attended and for two other churches in the area I would do the hospital visitation. When one of the members of any of those three churches was in the hospital, I would get a call to see if I would schedule to go and pray for the person that was in the hospital.

I got a call to go pray for a woman that was having trouble with her pregnancy. So, I called and made an appointment to see her later that day. I got to the hospital between 6-7 p.m. I found her room and when I came in, she was crying. I asked what the problem was. She shared that the doctor had just left and he had told her that he believed she needed to abort the baby. That if she didn't both her and the baby may die.

Then she began to tell me that she and her husband had wanted to have children for 10 years and they had tried everything, and she was now 35 years old and knew she was running out of time.

I suggested we pray and see what God has to say about this. (God is way bigger than this and we need to give Him the final word). We both prayed for a bit and she calmed down as God's peace rested on her!

There are different spiritual gifts that are mentioned in the Bible and they come to us as believers at different times for different reasons to allow God's presence and the power of His Spirit and Kingdom to break through into our reality. One of them is a word of knowledge where God speaks to our hearts with knowledge and information that we wouldn't otherwise know. And then it comes into our thought life, so we have the ability to communicate it to others.

It was at this time with this woman that the gift of knowledge came to me and God encouraged me to pass it on to her concerning what His plan was for her and her unborn child. So, I began to reveal to her what God had spoken to my heart.

She told me there was the slightest of chances that she could carry the baby to term, but due to her frailty and age the pregnancy may take a toll on her body and she may not recover from it. That is why the doctor encouraged her to terminate the pregnancy now while there was still time to do so. (She was six months pregnant the first time I came to the hospital to see her).

I told her what I believed God was asking of her. I told her if she would tell the doctor she was unwilling to terminate the pregnancy and that she would do whatever he told her to do in order to carry the baby full term. And that God Himself would stay with her to keep both her and the baby strong and healthy. She was going to spend the night at the hospital and the doctor was coming back in the morning to talk with her again. I told her I would come back in the morning to pray with her again.

I got there in the morning right after the doctor had left the room. She said the only way he would agree to her keeping her baby was to stay in the hospital on bed rest for the duration of the pregnancy and even then, he didn't think she would be able to do it. I asked her what did she think, could she do that? She said she had called her husband and told him all that had been said to her by the doctor and me. He told her it was her call and he would be there for her either way. So, I said let's pray. We prayed again and God's peace came on her again and she began to cry, she asked me what that was that was happening to her. I told her that was presence of God's peace letting her know that He was with her and for her and that He would keep His word to her and carry her and her unborn child through this. I told her I would come back twice a week every week until this was over.

I came back twice a week every week and the peace of God's presence came and rest on her each time we prayed. She was there in bed in the hospital for two and a half months then she gave birth to a strong, healthy baby girl. She stayed in the hospital for three days after the baby was born just to make sure she was strong enough to care for her new child. Then momma and baby were joined again with her husband, the new daddy. He had come to the hospital every night and brought his dinner with him and they had dinner every night as a family. Our God is an awesome God and has wonders to perform if we will just invite Him to the party and choose to trust Him rather than let fear or the opinions of others steal our joy.

Over the next few years God showed up many times in many ways with healing and blessings. I just can't remember specifics during this period of time. Skipping forward a few years to the next story, sorry that's the best my old, broken, torn up brain is capable of at this point in my life. I believe that is why my family and friends have asked me to write this book before I have lost more of the journey that I have been on. My wife and I now jokingly refer to my brain as the "Black Hole" now. Things go into it, but they never come back out.

Story #14

Lost but Not Forgotten

I was 29 or 30 and I had been working at a job that required me to drive long distances each day to get my work done. So, sometimes I was heading home after dark. This was one of those nights. I had about 30 more miles to get home. It was about 7 p.m. and dark and I needed gas to get the rest of the way home. I was putting gas into my truck and I saw a man sitting on the curb. This gas station was at the end of a street where there was a railroad trestle behind it. For years it was a hobo camp. They had access to food and a bathroom by staying there and no foot traffic so neither the hobos nor the people would bother each other. As I was finishing with filling my gas tank, I felt the Lord telling me to get the man that was sitting on the curb two chili dogs, a beer, and a pack of cigarettes. There had been many times over the past 14 years that God had asked me to buy people items, or pay their utility bills, but this was the first time I was asked to get beer and cigarettes. (I did not drink or smoke at that time in my life.)

I did a double check on that request as I pulled my truck away from the gas pump. Father are you sure you want me to get him those items. Then clear as day He said, "Get that man two chili dogs, a beer, and a pack of cigarettes." So, I went back into the Circle K and got two chili dogs out of the fridge and heated them in the microwave, went to the register and asked for a pack of cigarettes. The man at the register asked what kind and I said any, so he gave me Pall Mall Reds, I payed for them and walked towards the man on the curb.

When I got to him, I sat on the curb beside him and put my feet into the gutter next to his. I handed him the bag with the stuff in it. He said, "What's this." I said, God told me you needed this and told me to go buy it for you and give it to you." He opened the bag and inspected the content. Then he leaned back on one hand holding the bag in the other and asked me a question. "Who is your God?" I told him, "God the Father, Jesus His Son, and the Holy Spirit is the God I serve. Would you like to know Him?"

He said any God that would be so kind to a man like me is certainly a God I would like to know. So, I prayed with him right there in the gutter to have Jesus come and be the Lord of his life and that He would be a friend like no other, and that He wanted to share His life with him whatever that looked like. And that nothing could separate him from the love that God has for him. And that the power of His Kingdom and forgiveness would wash him clean and make him new. He began to sob. I put my arm around him for a minute and blessed him, told him he was my brother. He said, "I would like that."

I left as he was opening the chili dogs and the beer, and I began to drive home. About five minutes into my last leg home God spoke to me again, "Don't you want to know why I asked for those things." I answered honestly, "Yes, I really do. Why those things?" God said, "he is starving, he is also an advanced alcoholic. He will die without the food, without the grease in it and the beer to wash it down, he will throw it up. And the food will do him no good."

About 10 more minutes went by then I asked God, "What about the cigarettes? Why cigarettes?" A moment passed then God spoke, "He doesn't smoke, but he can trade them for food in the hobo camp he lives in and that pack of cigarettes will feed him for more than a week." I love my God, His compassion, kindness, and mercies have no end.

Story #15

The Father's Touch

I was 30 years old when I had the opportunity to go to England with my church to a group of pastors and church leaders. We were at Westminster Cathedral one night; I was walking the perimeter of the inside of the building as one my duties were to do a bit of security work and keep things peaceful.

Our pastor was teaching and as I walked, I believed I was supposed to stop and open a curtain that was up in the balcony. When I opened the corner of it, I saw a family. What appeared to be a mom and dad, a set of grandparents, and three young girls standing up leaning on the balcony rail. They looked in age to be about 12, 10, and 8 years old. God spoke to my heart and said, "If you will touch the little one, I will heal her." So, I eased my way through the few seats in front of me. I came up behind the little one. I just put one finger out and gently touched her on the back of her right shoulder. When I did, at that moment I touched her, she shouted out, "I can hear, I can hear." This disrupted the teaching. I went back to the curtain I had come through, turned around and looked down and about 100 feet below and away from me was my pastor looking at me with a big smile. He continued on teaching from where he had stopped. The parents calmed and quieted the child and I moved on.At the end of every day there, we would meet as a team to communicate all that God had done that day. Whenever someone was healed or a miracle would happen, someone would document the event. When the meeting was over the pastor came to me and asked if I knew what had happened up there. I told him, "not really."

He said after interviewing the parents they found out that the little girl had been born deaf and until that night had never heard. When I touched her, God came and healed her deafness. At the same moment, He did a miracle and gave her the ability to speak in the same language and dialect as her parents. With her never having heard she would not know how to speak. When she shouted out "I can hear, I can hear" my pastor's voice was the first voice she ever heard and when she shouted out, "I can hear, I can hear" those were the first words she ever spoke.

Many were healed and set free from demonic spirits during our time there; however, many of their stories are of a very personal nature and I will let them tell their own stories if and when they are ready to do so.

Story #16

The Velvet Glove

We went with another pastor and his wife with some other couples and our children to a different location about 30 miles from our existing church to plant and start another church. We were being sent out; we weren't just leaving on our own.

I was at this new church for a little over four years. After those four years, my wife and I separated, and I left the church at the pastor's request. So, I left. Both the separation from my wife and being asked to leave the church were as a result of my own doing. There is no fault or blame to any of them. My heart had grown cold, bitter, and selfish. I was angry and broken and was unwilling to change. I blamed God, it was all His fault and He didn't care enough to do anything about it. Lies, lies, lies. God and my family never stopped loving and caring for me. They were not going to let my rebellion and sin bring destruction to the church, themselves, or their families, or my family who were suffering the most.

I'm not sure how long it took for me to self-destruct. I believe it was only a matter of several months before I just gave up and wasn't willing to live in this condition anymore. So, I set out to end the pain. And that leads me to my next story and the second half of my life. (What was meant for evil, to harm me, God turned into good) not just for me but for everyone I knew and loved and who had to make many sacrifices to still love me with tough love.

There were even times when I pushed God Himself away and told Him to leave me alone. He was just a liar and a fraud. Once I even told him to "show His face so I could slap it and spit in His eye." Even at that, His love and the comfort of His presence never left me. Even when He finally needed to slap me down (to save my life), He did it with a velvet glove on His hand.

God is Faithful

I had decided to end my pain once and for all. I wasn't willing to commit suicide. If I did, my wife and children couldn't get my life insurance. At that time in the county I lived in had a zero-tolerance policy to bank robbery. So, I dressed up in a coat and tie and went to a bank that was only two miles down the street from one of the county sheriff's stations. I had a business card from an FBI Agent. I went to the vice president's desk and sat down. I handed him the card and told him that the card was mine and that I was armed, and he needed to go to the tellers and get me $10,000 in cash and bring it to me. I knew he had an alarm button at his desk. He said he would and got up and left. I stayed seated and waited for the police to get there. I could see the parking lot from the chair I was sitting in. In five minutes, there were 10 officers with weapons ready hiding behind several cars in the parking lot.

The Vice-President of the bank never returned, and I didn't think he would. I stood up to walk to the door and reach inside my jacket when I stepped out the door and let them end my pain. Just as I stood up the phone rang at the desk I had been sitting at. The vice-president from the teller's cage told me to answer it. It was for me.

I answered the phone and the man on the other end asked me who I was. He knew I wasn't the FBI Agent that I was pretending to be because he was the partner of that man and he had died from cancer a few months prior to this. I told him my real name and how I had gotten the card.

A year prior to this I had helped the FBI on a case of people stealing construction equipment and selling it at auction. I was in the construction equipment business at that time. He remembered me, he is a Christian man and he was out in the parking lot. He pleaded with me not to do this and asked if he could pray with me. I said yes and he said a short prayer that

God would come and open my eyes and heart to stop this insanity. Then he told me to "go to the door and drop my jacket out of the door and step out, put my hands behind my head and turn around and face the door." That's when I heard God's voice speak to me again as He had done so many times in the past. "It's time to surrender not just to them but to Me. I can redeem this, TRUST ME." And for the first time in a long time I had a moment of clarity. I did not really want to end my life this way. I just didn't want to live in the pain of the loneliness, sadness, and separation from all that I loved, which my intimacy with God was paramount.

So, I went to the door and did as the man on the other end of the phone had told me to do. I was hand cuffed and taken to jail. I was going to be charged with "Attempted Bank Robbery!!"

Story #18

I Gave Him My Yes

When I went before the judge, he postponed my trial and sent me to a drug and alcohol recovery program for 60 or 90 days, I don't remember which. I had started drinking when my wife and my church had told me to leave. Full of self-pity, feeling sorry for myself, and blaming all of them for the pain I was going through, I was about to get a huge dose of truth. God saved my life that day so that He could save it again and again as the years rolled by. He is and always will be faithful even when we are faithless. I was about to find out what "Mercy triumphs over judgement" really means. Thank you, Jesus, thank you, thank you.

While living at the rehab center I had to appear in court several times waiting for my turn to have the judge hear my case and saw many other people that had gone before the judge. He was the senior judge in my district, his nickname given to him by those that had been sentenced by him was "Hang Um High." He was no nonsense and showed no mercy. Many people that were first offenders like me (I had never been charged with a crime before) were getting 20 years or 20 years to life. A few got 40 years to life. When it finally was my turn I asked if I could go privately and just tell him and his court recorder what happened. God had already spoke to me to be brief and honest and trust Him for the results. So, that's what I did. We went into his chambers and I told him everything that happened and all that I had done. When I was finished, he told me to come back in a week and he would have a ruling.

So, I went back to the rehab center and waited. God spoke to me again during that week and told me to accept what the judge was going to say and trust Him for the results. I went back to the court in a week and the judge found me guilty of attempted bank robbery and he sentenced me to five years. Then said I had 30 days to put my affairs in order, then self-surrender to the Marshalls to start my time. I went to my parent's home to stay with them for the 30 days. I had an opportunity to say good bye to my kids and told them I would be back and that I loved them and that I would do whatever I could to get out as soon as I could and that I would write them and send them cards. At that time my son was 12 years old and my daughter was only nine years old. At the end of my 30 days I went to the U.S. Marshall's office that was in the town my parents lived in. They took me to a detention center in Los Angeles to wait for me to be designated to a prison. I was the only one out of at least 40 cases I heard that got such a small sentence. The federal guidelines at that time were 10 years to life. My judge departed downwards from the guidelines by half. ("Surely His goodness and mercy will follow us all the days of our lives.") That is just who He is.

Story #19

Waiting on God

I spent the next four and a half years in prison. The next several stories are part of what God did when He showed up behind those prison walls. After turning myself into the Federal Marshall's I was taken to a holding facility to wait for my designated prison where I would serve out my sentence.

After being there for a week or so, I was assigned to mopping the floors at night. I overheard two of the guards talking and one was telling the other about his son (a young boy) who had recently been diagnosed with spinal meningitis. I remembered about eight years prior to this time, our friend's wife was diagnosed with the same illness. We had gathered family and friends at our home, and we all prayed for her. God came and we believed she was healed. She went to her specialist a week later and it was confirmed that she was healed.

So, I told the officer I had overheard his conversation about his son. I told him the story of our friend's wife and asked if I could pray for his son. He said, "yes." I invited the Holy Spirit to come and empower the officer's hands and give him the courage and faith to put his hands on his son when he got home and pray for a miracle. I told him I would continue to pray until his son went back to the doctor. I didn't hear anything from the officer for about 10 days. I had already gotten orders that I would be leaving to go to my designated prison the next day.

There was a tap on my cell door about 2 a.m. It was the officer with the sick son. He told me that after praying for his son they had gotten more test done and that they had come back negative. And that God had healed his son.

Story #20

God Heals Cancer

When I got to my prison of designation after about a week, I heard one of the sergeants talking to one of the correctional officers in the chow hall about his wife having cancer. I began to pray and ask God if I was supposed to ask to pray for his wife with him.

I didn't see him again for about two weeks. Again, I saw him in the chow hall. I asked to speak to him. I told him of the other officer's son and how God had healed him of spinal meningitis and asked if I could pray with him for his wife who had brain cancer. He told me, "not here." I said, "okay."

Two days later about midnight my cell door opened up. It was the sergeant. He told me he and his wife were both Christians and he would welcome prayer. I took a new handkerchief out of my drawer and the two of us prayed over it. I suggested he put it on her head when she was going to go to bed and put his hands on it and pray over her. I told him I would continue to pray until I heard back from him. I did not see him or hear from him for a couple of weeks.

My work detail was in the construction part of the prison. We went all over the prison painting and repairing things. I found out shortly that the officer in charge of our work detail was a Christian. I carried a pocket size New Testament with me and read it whenever we had down time. My supervisor asked me to stay for a minute after our work detail was dismissed. When everyone else left he told me the sergeant that I had prayed with, had contacted him and told him that when his wife had gone to the cancer treatment center, they retested her to prepare a treatment program for her and the cancer was gone along with the tumors. God is so good; He doesn't care who we are or what our status is in life. He is full of mercy and compassion and He has wonders to perform.

Story #21

Psalms 102:19 & 20

There was an inmate about 30 years old. He had been an addict and he was battling HIV that he had picked up using a dirty needle. The HIV had advanced to become full blown AIDS. He worked as the office tech in our construction division at the prison. He was down to 85 pounds when they confined him to the prison hospital. The prison knew he was dying and were going to transfer him to the BOP Hospital. I asked my supervisor if he could get me into the hospital to see him before he was transferred. He said he would try. Two days later he told me to prepare a cart to paint at the hospital unit (I knew he was going to get me in to see my friend). When we got there, he let me into his isolation room and told me I had 20 minutes.

I prayed and asked the Father what I was supposed to do. How was I to pray? My friend had sores all over his face and body and God told me to "clean his sores and get him ready to leave!" So, I put rubber gloves on, and God told me, "No, take the gloves off. Then clean him." I was reminded of Jesus touching lepers and staying clean. So, I figured the Father would protect me also. So, I cleaned him, and I prayed for him. My friend slept through the whole thing. In my heart I believed I was preparing him for death. I prayed that he would find peace with God and be free of fear. He was a black man that grew up in the projects, he knew what fear was.

He was transported later that day to the BOP hospital. Later that night about midnight my cell was opened, and I was told to get dressed. I did and was chained and shackled and taken to the warden. The warden asked me what I had done to my friend. I told him I cleaned him and put ointment on his sores. He yelled at me and said, "you prayed for him, didn't you?" I replied, "yes, I did." He then said, "I warned you about that" which he had, a couple of times. I said, "what happened? Did he die?" The warden replied, "no, when he arrived at the hospital, he had gained 25 lbs. and there were no more sores on his body and he no longer has HIV." I said, "Praise God." The warden then ordered me to be put in the hole. (I had been forbidden "to put my hands-on people and pray). The hole is a row of cells that are six feet by six feet with a concrete bench, a stainless-steel toilet and sink and that's it. The lights are controlled from the outside. So, if they want you in the dark, you are. And if they want you in the light, you are.

This was not the first time I was sent to the hole nor would it be the last. In total I spent 30 days in the hole nine different times and every time it was for inviting the power or peace and the presence of the Living God to show up. I was transferred many times and put in the hole every time I got some where new for disobeying a direct order 'not to pray'.

A senior officer or warden would come interview me there and ask, "If I was going to be a problem." I would always answer by saying, "If you mean by being a problem, am I going to pray? The answer is yes."

I had "diesel therapy" once. (That is when you travel shackled with wrist chains, ankle chains, and belt chains connecting them) by bus all over the country staying in county jails for days or weeks and staying in other prisons for days, weeks, or up to a month then move on somewhere else. You receive no mail and have no access to phones. It is a form of punishment when you have done nothing wrong except displease the powers that be.

A warden in a prison here in this country when I was in them over 30 years ago was no different than a king or queen of a third world country. They have the authority to have you beaten, put in isolation, put with violent offenders, who had the permission of the powers that be, to harm you at will or even have you killed, if they so desired.

Story #22

When God Shows Up

I am very blessed that I only had to deal with this once. God had given me an opportunity to pray with a couple members of the Black Panthers who were doing life without parole. They both prayed to accept Christ and found great joy in the grace and forgiveness of God. One of the leaders of The Aryan Brotherhood found out that I showed respect and kindness to all.

Color, race, nationality, or position they made no difference. God is not a respecter of persons, and neither was I. He had let it be known that if he could get to me, he would kill me. This Aryan Brotherhood inmate was a large man and had already killed other men he was incarcerated with.

My unit was out on a ramp waiting to get into the commissary. I could hear commotion behind me. And I looked back and saw his 6'8" 380 lb. frame on the other side of a locked gate. The officer was taking off his shackles and was unlocking the gate. When the gate opened, he was coming down the ramp heading straight for me.

I will never forget the prayer I prayed that day for I had never prayed it before that day or since. There was about 80 feet between he and I and he was closing quickly. I said, "Father, you are going to have to do something or I am going to have to kill that man." (I have never been put in a situation where I had to take the life of another human being and wasn't ever sure I would be able to justify doing such a thing.) However, that was my prayer. When he got about 30 feet from me, his body went up about 10 feet to the left about 10 feet and backwards about 15 feet where his body slammed into a brick building knocking him out.

It was my turn to go into the commissary and I went in and got my stuff. This only took a couple of minutes coming back to get back to my unit and back to my cell two officers were attending to the man that had sworn he would kill me. He was awake but still on the ground.

Thank you, sweet Jesus that I never had to deal with anything like that again. (It reminded me of the time when the donkey spoke to the Prophet "asking why are you beating me telling me to move forward don't you see the angel standing in front of you with his sword drawn read to take off your head." I don't believe this man saw the angel between he and I. But when he encountered God's power all his size and strength and rage amounted to less than nothing. The presence of the Kingdom of God threw him like he was a tiny rag doll.

Story #23

You Can't Keep God Out

One of the inmates that worked in the kitchen at one of the prisons I was in came to me out on the ball field and told me about one of his homies that was in the hole. He had just received a letter and found out his infant daughter had been diagnosed with stomach cancer. The homie in the hole told him to find me and ask me to pray for her. I told the man who had asked me to pray to meet me on the ball field the next day. I wrote down a prayer and told him to tell his homie to send it to his wife and have her pray that prayer over their baby. I continued to pray the same prayer over the baby for over a month. (When you are in the hole, mail is slower going out and slower still coming back in if they are willing to give it to you at all).

The inmate that worked in the kitchen found me out on the rec yard and told me the baby's momma prayed the prayer over choir practice at the Baptist Church that her and her extended family attended and she had made copies of the prayer for all of them to read and they all read it together. The following week when they took the baby to the doctor the test came back clean and the cancer was gone.

Just a note, during the four and a half years I was in prison I was able to pray with hundreds of people. All colors, races, from 20 different countries, at least 10 different religions and I have to say that God's grace, mercy, kindness, and power know no boundaries. I even saw Him heal a professed atheist.

However, there were many more that weren't healed and many more that didn't want to give their lives to Christ. I've been called every name there is and threatened. But it isn't about me or even those who had prayer offered to them. It's about obeying the will of God. He said in His Word "pray without stopping, in everything give thanks." And one of my favorites "Above all else, love each other deeply, for love covers a multitude of sins." I have learned that it is not about what we know, what we believe or even what we are able to teach. It is about what we are willing and committed "TO DO ABOUT IT." We are to be doers of His word and not just hearers of it.

Story #24

Pushing Through the Pain

There were a couple of times when God showed up to heal me personally. But those can wait for another time. There were two other times in prison I needed to have surgery. This story is about one of those times.

Whenever an inmate needs to leave the prison, the Warden has to sign off before you can go for surgery (even if it is considered an emergency). I had a hemorrhoid and it was acute in the course of trying to use the toilet the hemorrhoid ruptured, and I was bleeding a lot. I was taken to the prison hospital and they said I needed emergency surgery. I packed my bottom with Vaseline and a sock trying to slow down the bleeding.

At this time, I was back in the prison with the warden that did not like me at all. I waited a whole day and was still bleeding. I checked with the unit manager the next morning and still no word from the warden. I was on phone restriction at the time, but I knew I needed to talk to my dad. There was a man in our unit that would sell his phone time to inmates like me that were on phone restriction. He had three way calling at his home. He would call his home collect (all calls from prison at that time were collect) and then he would have his wife dial the number that the inmates needed, and we could connect with our families.

I was able to get ahold of my dad on the phone. I told him what was going on and did he have any ideas of what I could do. He said he would do what he could. (I had no clue what that meant. He also told me to keep doing what I was doing).

I was taken for surgery that night, but I didn't find out for a couple of weeks what exactly had occurred. My dad had served in the Army with a man who had become a Congressman. My dad called him and told him my story and asked if he could help. That Congressman at the time happened to be on the Appropriations Committee. He got on the phone to the director of the BOP and told him if he wanted to see any money for their budget, he had better call my warden and he had better get me in for emergency surgery ASAP. And that is how I got the surgery that kept me from bleeding to death.

There is an important reason that I tell this story. It is not always the supernatural or the miraculous that is needed to allow God to work in our lives. Sometimes it takes us being willing to reach out and tell those God has placed in our lives of the need we have and asking for their help. We all need to be sensitive to "be the kind of friend, a friend would like to have."

God uses people all the time to get His purposes done. Be aware and willing the next time someone asks you if you can help (It might not be something that saves a life) but it for sure can be something that makes a difference in the lives of those who are asking for your help. Never discount prayer. My heart is wounded when I hear people say, "All I could do was pray." Prayer is always the place I start. The Lord our God in our midst is mighty – He will save.

You Can't Hide from God

I was getting short on my prison term. I had six months left to do. One day I was called to my unit manager's office. When I got there several people were in there waiting for me. The Sargent, who was a believer, was the one doing the talking. He was the one who asked for the meeting. He told me he was certain that one of the other correctional officers had brought a gun loaded and sold it to one of the inmates. They knew who the inmate was but didn't know where he had hidden the gun in the prison. The sergeant asked me to pray (it was his wife that had been healed of cancer) and ask God if He would tell me where the gun is and recover it before someone or several people were killed. I told them I would pray and ask God to take this threat up off of us all.

I prayed for two days then the Holy Spirit spoke to me clearly. (It's in the kitchen). I told my counselor who was also in that meeting that I needed my work duty changed to the kitchen. She asked if it was related to that meeting. I answered, "Yes." The next day I was assigned to the bakery. As I was there working, I kept asking God where it was. The next day He told me to look up as I was at the sink washing out large sheet cake pans. When I looked up, I saw one of the ceiling panels a little cock eye. I was sure God was telling me the gun was in there.

The head of the kitchen said he needed a volunteer to come in early the next day to make blue berry muffins. I volunteered to come in at 3 a.m. I knew I would be alone in the kitchen for over an hour. I pulled one of the eight-foot-long stainless-steel tables over to the sink and got up on it and pushed the ceiling panel out of the way and started feeling around. I felt something hard in a plastic bag. I grabbed it and pulled it out, it was the gun. I quickly put the table back and hid the gun in the pantry behind the 50 lb. bags of flour. After breakfast was served, I looked for something to hide it in. There was an empty five-pound coffee can and I took it to the pantry and put the gun in it.

The next day was Wednesday. That was the day they take out the huge trash compactor to the dump. Just before my shift ended,

I was escorted with the trash from the bakery out to the compactor. I had put the coffee can in an empty 50 lb. flour bag. The next morning, I waited until the trash compactor was outside the guarded gate. Then I asked if I could go to my cell because I needed to get meds. I went to my counselor and told her the gun had left the prison and was on its way to the dump. I told her to call and tell them "not to dump it" until there were officers from the prison to sort through the trash so they could recover the gun and what I had put it in so it would be easy to find. I was called out of work the next day to go see the unit manager. (He told me they had recovered the gun). (Representatives from the prison could get there. I told her it would be at the very back of the load as they pushed the trash out of it and that it was in a flour sack in a coffee can). As a perk he told me they would transfer me to any prison I wanted to go to. At that time there was only one prison close enough to my children that I would be able to get a visit from them. I picked there. That prison was a large concrete box in a metropolitan area with no outside yard!! He said, "Are you sure that's where you want to go?" I said, "Yes sir." This place was about 60 miles from my kids. A week later I was 600 miles closer to my kids and hoping to get a visit.

Story #26

Mercy Triumphs Over Judgement

This will be my last prison story as this one is the one God used to walk me out the doors of that place. Although there are several more to tell I can't do any more. To relive that season of my life has been brutally painful. I have dismissed that whole time from the day I walked out of that hell hole. In fact, the night I was being released one of the guards that was preparing me for release stepped up to me and said, "You will never forget your inmate number, and you will be back." The inmate number is an inventory number because you are the property of the Federal Government and a large percentage of people leaving prison become repeat offenders and end up back in prison. It is called "the revolving door." I remember telling him, "you will never see me again and I will forget that number within 30 days." And as it turned out in three weeks' time, I couldn't remember my inmate number (or inventory number – I was no longer their property).

Now to tell the story. I was impressed by the Holy Spirit to write my sentencing judge a letter and tell him all that God had done during the time that I had spent in prison. I prayed about it for a couple of weeks as I really didn't want to. I had the impression that this was important and needed to be done. So, I put pen to paper and listed all the prison programs that I completed and other work that was done during the four and a half years I was in there. At the end of the letter I thanked him again for "tempering justice with mercy" the same as I did the day he sentenced me. I took it to my counselor as it was to be mailed "Legal Mail." All legal mail had to be sent out this way. Legal mail was not allowed to be read before it left the prison. All other mail could not be sealed and was read before being mailed. All mail coming into the prison was opened and read before being delivered except for legal mail; you had to get it from your counselor and open it and let them view the content without reading it.

A couple of weeks later I was called to the counselor's office for legal mail pick up. I opened it and it was the letter I had sent to the sentencing judge. However, it had a couple of rubber stampings at the top of the first page of the three pages with dates and signatures on them. There was one page from the court with a couple sentences written on it. One of the stamps read "Post-Conviction Acquittal Motion" with a date and the signature of the clerk of his court. The second stamp read "granted" and was signed by my judge. On the piece of paper from the court it read "This man is acquitted of all charges and is hereby ordered to be released from custody forthwith. All charges against him are hereby stricken from his record." I read this in front of my counselor and asked her what this meant. She said the judge converted the letter you sent him into a "Post-Conviction Acquittal Motion then he stamped it "Granted and signed it." That means you are free to go and these charges against you have been dismissed. This didn't come to me until late on a Friday afternoon. By the time the prison could get all the paperwork done and get me ready to be released it was late on the following Monday. They knew they had to have me out of the prison by 10 p.m. on that Monday or they would be in contempt of court. I left the prison that Monday night at 9:59 p.m. They got every last minute out of me. I have not been charged with a crime since and still can't remember my inmate number and I left there over 25 years ago.

Story #27

Free at Last

Now, moving on! The night I was released from prison they did not give me my money or my property, they said they were going to mail it to my parent's house (that was the address I gave them as my new place of residence). I was dressed in a pair of sweatpants a size too small and a woman's sweater (their way of final disrespect and devaluing to cause me to feel less than human). I went to the gas station across the street from the prison and asked if I could use their phone to make a collect call. They said, "Yes." I called my dad and told him I had been released and could he come and get me. The prison was about 35 miles from their home. He said to just stay where I was, and he would take care of it.

About 15 minutes later a taxi pulled up and asked if I was Dave. I had told my dad what I was wearing and how ridiculous I looked. My dad must have told the Cab Company what I was wearing. The cab took me to my parent's house, and they paid the cab for me. I borrowed a pair of his sweats and a t-shirt and flannel. It was 11 p.m. by now and I told my parents I would be back in less than an hour. I walked down the sidewalk for about a mile and then turned around and walked back, looking at the trees in the park, listening to the dogs barking, smelling the smells of "FREEDOM." I began to cry and thank my sweet Jesus for His love, kindness, mercy, and the generosity of His compassion. Shortly after getting out of prison my dad asked if I would like to partner with him and open a construction company, so he did all the paperwork and got the licenses we needed, and we were in business.

Story #28

Give All You've Got

We mostly worked in and around the town where my parents lived. We were doing a roof repair about five miles from their home and a woman from across the street came over and asked if I would come over when I was done for the day. She had some work and wanted to know if we would be able to do it for her. At the end of the day I went over to talk to her. (Just a note: I have thought of this couple and their children and purpose for over 25 years and prayed for them often and shared their story over and over again. I love them and they are remarkable).

When I came in the house it was full of special needs children, some very severe. One little guy wanted me to pick him up so I asked if I could. She said, "Sure." I picked him up and he gave me a huge, long hug. I carried him while we talked. Most of what she wanted done was normal wear and tear and maintenance, except for a 20-foot-long handicap ramp coming from the front door to the middle of the front yard. And a large treacherous bougainvillea that needed to be removed in the back yard to make a safe play area for the kids.

This remarkable couple had just bought the house and it was going to be their home and they were sharing it with their adopted children. All nine of their children had special needs of one kind or another and one of the children was in a reclined wheelchair. She couldn't walk or speak. But I soon found if you smiled at her and touched the side of her face gently, she would smile and wiggle from side to side and make the loveliest moaning sounds.

My dad mostly did paperwork and ran the business end of our company. After I had been working at this home for a couple of days I would come home and tell my dad about these women and their incredible family. He said, "Well, I'm going with you tomorrow. We headed over there about 7:30 a.m. I had told him when we get there one of the moms is going to open the front door and a little guy is going to come running once he gets down the stairs so "be ready." We got out of the truck and the screen swung open and here came this little six-year-old boy with a smile as big as the sky itself. He put his face right between my dad's thighs and wrapped his arms around my dad's legs and almost knocked my dad to the ground. (My dad was 6 ft. tall and weighed about 180 lbs. at that time.) I picked him up and carried him back in the house with the others. I introduced my dad to the mom that had been at the door. My dad said, "I think I know you." She asked if he had ever eaten at a little restaurant in town. He said, "Yes, I love that place." She said, "I opened it and owned it for years. I sold it to be one of the moms of this crew." My dad looked around at the nine kids and their special conditions and he teared up just like I did. Both moms are white, and all their adopted children are black. Because of their condition they bounced around the foster care system until these incredible women took a stand and adopted them all from different foster homes.

They had a set of twin girls maybe nine or 10 years old. They didn't appear to have the same disabilities that the others had. The two of them were precious and wanted to help. We brought the material that day to start on the ramp. So, after we unloaded the truck, we brought them out. (Their little brother sat on the other side of the locked screen in order not to miss a thing). Yet we could only keep him safe locked in the house.

We handed the speed squares and framing pencils to the girls. We would measure and mark the wood and they would draw the straight line for us to cut. When it was time to put it together, I would hold the lumber in place and my dad would hold the nail gun while they pulled the trigger. It was an awesome, amazing day that day. We finished the ramp the next day. When we got there, the third day and the mom opened the door, her son came to greet us with such speed, I had to run towards him to catch him so that he'd not nosedive face first. He was laughing so hard and wanted me to put him down so he could do it again.

I asked one of the moms to come out after we had put the boy in the house. I asked her what was wrong with the twins. She said they both have a rare cancer that is untreatable and they will die in a year or two. I started to cry (they are both so beautiful and smart and kind). We asked if we could pray with her for them and she said, "Sure." My dad is more a private prayer person so I prayed and asked God to open heaven and send His angels to this place and send one for each of them – all nine children and both moms. (I am certain He did, and that house was full of more joy and peace than any I've ever been in.)

When we finished the rest of the work, I told my dad I didn't want to charge them anything for our labor and my dad agreed. When we told them this, they weren't having it. My son had just got his driver's license at that time and they had an old Ford LTD out in the back. My son needed a car. We said how about we trade the labor for the car (It was the same age as my son.) They said, "We would love that, we wanted to sell it anyway!"

My dad was an excellent mechanic. We took the car to his house. It only needed a few minor repairs and four new tires. In a few days it was ready to be picked up, and my dad called for him to pick up his car. That car was like a tank, I was so peaceful for him to drive it. If he were to get in an accident, he and the people in his car were going to be safe. A few years later I found out from my daughter that all the kids including them called the car "The Banana Boat."

My dad died of brain cancer less than a year after we had the privilege of sharing part of our journey with this incredible family. We stayed in touch with them. The twins died within a year of each other a couple years after my dad died.

When my dad and I would talk of the experiences and adventures we shared with that special family, we were always left with a smile on our faces (I know "Angels Walk Among Us"). We met 11 of them at that home and prayed down 11 more to carry and comfort them and provide love, joy, peace, and courage for the rest of their journey.

Story #29

Invite God to the Party

I am at about 42 right now (in this book) and God is telling me to speak freely of myself. I don't want any of you reading this to think or believe that I am some kind of mountain goat that just leaps from mountain top to mountain top, and victory to victory and glory to glory. Because I'm NOT. Between the ages of 40 and 56, I lived in 15 different homes in four different states. My wife of 20 years divorced me just before I left prison because she wasn't sure what kind of man I may have become. Prison changes people some for better and some for worse. She is a godly woman and was going to make sure my 16-year-old son and my 13-year-old daughter were safe and protected, and she herself needed to live in peace. I supported her choice then and still do. God told her to do that. Many of you believers may think that is not Biblical, just keep reading and you will see what God is doing. (Our precious Lord is way bigger than His Book.) And He didn't stop talking to people once those pages were written. Intimacy with His Person and His Presence have just as much wisdom and direction as His Word. Before I get in trouble, I have read the whole Bible from cover to cover over 40 times. I have read 10,000's of pages of Biblical Commentaries Bible Dictionary of both Hebrew and Greek. At one time I had more than half the New Testament memorized. Now that I'm retired, I spend hours each day at my home on my porch worshipping, praying, petitioning, praying in the Spirit. The intimacy we experience together every day is like being on a never ending incredible, breath taking, vacation with my best friend whom I love, and who loves me so much more than I even can express. I run out of words of gratitude and praise for Him and I just weep and groan.

I also still read His word every day. I have done that (mostly) for the past 50 years. I've been on a good course for the past 10 years, but for the 14 year before there was a lot of dry time. Paul spent 14 years in the desert after God called him. Moses spent 40 years in the wilderness after he murdered a man. David committed adultery then ordered the husband of the woman to be set up to be murdered. God never leaves. He walks through the whole journey with us, He conquers our shame. He's the lifter of our heads. (there were times I was looking up through the bottom), yet His love and mercy were present even there. No matter how dark a place I created for myself by my poor choices, He was there with the light and glory of His mighty presence. It was His love that was poured out to ransom all our souls. Our debt, all of us, was paid by Him with the price of His blood and death. Now He lives to give every last person on this planet life, the joy of His Hope, the peace You left with us to live in us! (That great and glorious Holy Spirit.) "It's all about You, Jesus, it's all about You."

Thank you for your patience, which I rambled on for a few minutes. I ask for a little more. I think all of this can be summed up in two verses, one from the Old Testament and one from the New Testament. Ezra 7:10 says, "I have studied your laws and precepts and I have hidden them in my heart so that I might DO THEM, then teach in all of Israel." It is not what you believe or what you know, or even what you might feel qualified to teach. What counts is what YOU DO ABOUT IT. What is the message of your life? Others will know whom you believed in and what you believe by how your life is lived out. The verse in the New Testament is just as powerful. 1 Peter 4:8: "Above ALL ELSE LOVE each other deeply. LOVE covers a multitude of sin." If we choose to give the Father's love away as generously as He has given it to us, His forgiveness, mercy, grace, kindness, compassion, comfort, and peace, there is no end to the joy and happiness we hold in our hearts and hands as we reach them out in His name for His Glory. Invite Him to the party even if it's just a party of two. He will show up and He will be the 800 lb. gorilla in the room. When He shows up everything changes.

Story #30

How Much God Loves

From now through the rest of the stories will not be in any kind of chronological order that is just not how my brain works. In taking the notes to put this together, I wrote down events when I remembered them, and they were all over the place. If I don't follow my notes there is no telling what might happen. It is my belief that all the stories that are in my notes need to be told and I don't want to forget to put them in here. My wife calls my brain the black hole. "Things go into it, but they don't come out." I tell people my brain in not my friend even though it is attached to my body.

I do not drive and haven't for several years. While I was still healthy enough, I would ride the buses all over the county where I live in to get where I needed to go (now my family and friends give me rides.) On one of the days I was taking the bus I was waiting at the bus stop connecting from one bus to a different one. I had just come from the Dr. I was told at the Dr. that I had skin cancer all over. They would be able to burn off 30 of the tumor spots buy there were 12 on my back and head that would require two surgeries to remove all of them.

As I was sitting on the bench pondering the information I had just received, the weather changed rapidly, and it began to rain, and in a few minutes, it was raining hard. I had only a t-shirt and shorts on (it was supposed to be a sunny day). I bowed my head and asked God in exasperation, ("Father would you please do something about this? I really don't need this right now!") In a moment of time all around the bench I was sitting on stopped raining. Not only did this little 10' x 10' area stop raining (while it was still raining hard as far as I could see just beyond this) I was dry and so was the bench and the ground around it. As I looked to my left, I saw an older woman digging through the trash can there. She was about 30 ft. from me. She also was not dressed properly for this heavy rain. So, I asked God again for His help. "Father, could you please push this a little to the west so that woman won't be wet and risk getting sick?" Again, in a moment of time the areas around her as well as a 4 ft. wide strip between her and I wasn't raining, and the ground was dry. It was still raining hard as far as I could see, and I began to thank my great and mighty God for the generosity of His kindness. As I told Him how grateful I was He spoke to me again, ("How grateful are you?") He had spoken those words to me before many times and I knew what He meant. I said in return, "Father, I only have a dollar" (as though God didn't know that already) and then He said, "That's all she needs." So, I got up from the bench and walked over to the trash can, she was bent all the way from the waist up down into the trash can. I had the dollar in my hand. I pushed my hand down into the trash can with the dollar bill in my hand and said to her, "here, God said you needed this." She reached her hand up and took the bill from my hand without saying a word. As I stepped away to walk back to the bench to wait for my bus, the woman began to cry (still remaining face down in the trash can.) When I sat down on the bench I prayed again. "Father, should I have waited and asked if I could pray for her?" and God spoke again. "Son she is not crying because you gave her the dollar. She is crying because when you gave it to her, I stuck my head into the trash can, kissed her on the cheek and reminded her of my love for her, and how special she is to me."

When I heard those words in my heart, I began to cry then weep. As I sat there on that bus bench thinking how the King of everything, the Lord of the impossible, the God of creation came to this obscure place on His planet and put His glorious head into a stinky, funky, trash can to give a kiss to an old homeless woman for the purpose of leaving His love, kindness, and hope as her covering. I was overwhelmed and left completely undone.

My bus arrived and as I got on, I was still crying. The driver was a young black woman (we knew each other by name, I rode that bus a lot. It was the last bus coming from anywhere in the county that would drop me off near my home). She asked me "Dave, are you alright?" I said, "I just found out I have skin cancer and am going to need more surgeries. I also just saw a miracle from God, and it makes the cancer seem insignificant. These tears are tears of joy and gratitude for a loving Father that never gives up on us." She gave me a hearty, heartfelt amen and let me know she would be praying for me!!!

Story #31

Miracle Worker

I had gone into the hospital for a minor surgery on my left foot. I was to spend the night and go home the next day. When talking with the young surgeon that had assisted in the surgery, I pointed out to him that my wound seemed to be infected. He responded by saying, "if I were the attending doctor in the emergency room and you came in with this infection, I would tell you it is no big deal and I would send you home." So, we went home. The next morning, I woke up and looked at my foot. A pocket of pus larger than a golf ball had formed on my foot and a two-inch-wide red streak was halfway up the front of my left shin bone going towards my knee. We went straight to the E.R. and that same young doctor happened to be there. I looked at him straight in the eye and said, "How about now? Is it a big deal now? Just cut my leg off below the knee so I can save the rest of my leg. And when I get through with you, you will never practice medicine anywhere again. And you are not allowed to touch me again or I will sue this hospital as well as you personally."

I was prepped for emergency surgery; my wife was there. She told me I had been infected with a VISA Mersa Staph Infection and that I was going to need more surgery. Again, I told them to cut the lower part of my leg off. Over the next five weeks I had 11 surgeries. One evening I woke up from another surgery. (The whole time I was in the hospital I was in a building out in the parking lot called the Infectious Disease Ward). Across the room was a Hispanic man. His three daughters and wife were there with his doctor. I heard the doctor say to them "to say their goodbyes to him that he wouldn't live through the night. The doctor and the wife walked out of the room together. The three girls about 13, 11, and 9 years old were at their father's bedside. All were crying quietly. At that moment our Sweet Jesus caused faith to rise up in me. He said, "Just believe, he won't die." As the girls started to leave the room the oldest to the youngest, I spoke out to the youngest one and asked her to come close to my bed. She walked right up to me with tears still coming down her cheeks.

I told her that God Himself had just come into the room and that He said, "That her father was not going to die, that He was going to raise him up, and we just needed to believe and trust Him." I told her, "Your dad isn't going to die tonight." She smiled and ran out of the room. When my wife and pastor got there that night, I told them they needed to go pray for that man. They said, "We will after we pray for you." I stopped them and told them what had happened earlier with his doctor and family, and what God had spoken. They agreed they would go pray for him first. They asked him if they could pray for him. He said it would be okay. They prayed for a few minutes and then came back over to my bed to pray for me. Before they finished praying for me, he was sitting up in his bed. He called for the nurse and told them the pain was gone and he could breathe freely. My wife and pastor left after praying for me. The nurses came in and checked the man in the other bed. They called for the doctors to come in.

The next morning, they ran a bunch of tests on that man. He was totally healed. He called his wife and she came with his girls to get him. As they were all leaving together the littlest one that I had spoken with the night before ran over to me and hugged me and said, "I prayed, me and my sisters and my mom. We all prayed together." I told her, "God heard your prayer honey and He has given you back your father." The dad came over and thanked me, I told him, "Oh thank your sweet Jesus. He loves you and stands with you." The little one hugged me again and they left.

I was scheduled for another surgery. After I woke up from this one my ex-wife was at my bedside praying for me. (She is a powerful, godly woman and I know she hears God). I reached my hand out and touched her forearm which startled her. She did not know I had woken up from the surgery. I asked, "What is God saying because we got nothing!!" She told me that she and the other ladies in her prayer group have been getting the same word "that mercy triumphs over judgement."

I went back out again and when I woke up again, she was gone. When my wife came later in the early evening after she got off work, I told her what had happened that day and asked her what she thought of the "word" given meant. She didn't hesitate and she said, "I think we are supposed to forgive the hospital, and the surgeon, and everyone that may have taken part in this." (We had already been contacted by a couple of lawyers wanting to sue the hospital on our behalf.)

We prayed right then and forgave them all. We both had a great peace at that moment. The next day two of my surgeons came in to see me and asked if I was going to sue the other surgeon and the hospital because of what had just occurred. I told them, "No, have that young surgeon come see me" (he had respected my wishes when I was admitted a month earlier to stay away from me). Later that afternoon he came to see me. I told him that we had forgiven him and the hospital for what had happened. (I did give him a stern admonishment that he needed to listen to his patients and not dismiss what they are telling him without investigating their condition.") When my wife got to the hospital the next evening, we prepared a release of liability for the hospital, surgeons, and any and all other parties. We put it in writing and signed off on it.

My last surgery of that stay was in the morning. (When we gave mercy, instead of pursuing judgement, it was over, well almost over). A couple of days later they were preparing to release me from the hospital after five weeks of being there. As my wife was pushing me in a wheelchair, she stopped the doctor and asked, "What can we expect? No one has given us any information as to when my husband might be up again?" The doctor responded, "he will need three or four skin grafts to replace the top of his foot that we had to remove, we also removed several bones in whole or in part, your husband won't be able to walk on his own power ever again." That was it for me. I put the brakes on the wheelchair. I took my wife's hand and pulled myself up and said, "Oh hell no, my God is just way bigger than that." I took a couple of steps. They ran and grabbed some crutches. And I walked out of the hospital. It took God about three or four weeks to grow all the skin back on the top of my foot with no skin grafts. They said it wasn't possible and that my God is a miracle worker!

Story #32

Give His Love Away

I was on a county bus coming back from the foot doctor who was monitoring my healing. The bus was getting close to where I get off the bus. So I moved from the back (where I prefer to sit) to the front of the bus to be able to exit easily.

When I sat down, I noticed the woman sitting right across the aisle from me. (She was about 10 years younger than me). She was bald from chemo, had some teeth missing, was a little dirty, and was talking to someone on her cell phone. When she ended the call, I reached my hand across the aisle and said, "Hi, my name is Dave; what's yours?" She stuck her hand out and took mine in hers and told me her name. I held onto her hand and I asked her if I could pray for her, she said yes.

I took her hand and wrapped it in both my hands, and I prayed a short prayer "that the love of the Father would come and bring hope and comfort to this wonderful woman." When I finished praying, she had tears running down her cheeks. I was still holding onto her hand. Then she spoke!! "Do you know how long it has been since anyone has touched me? I know I'm dirty and I stink, but I have feelings too, you know!" Her words and the pain and loneliness that resounded with them cut right through my heart and soul. I responded to her declaration with these words "Oh yes you do honey and that is why the presence of the true and living God is here on this bus right now in all His Glory, the King of everything. He is here to let you know how precious you are and how deeply he loves you." Then I let her hand go. With tears coming down her cheeks she picked up her phone and made a call. When the person on the other end of the phone answered she said, "God just showed up on the bus and told me that He loves me" then hung up, dialed another number when they answered she said, "God showed up on the bus and told me that he loves me." (That time her face was full of joy). She hung up and began to make another call.

The bus had arrived at my stop. I got up and started to exit the bus. I was sitting right behind the driver. When I stepped forward the driver grabbed the pole so I couldn't exit. This bus driver could have easily been a defensive tackle in the NFL. He was about 6'6", weighing about 300 lbs. (I am not a small man myself). At that time in and around the county I live in there was some racial tension going on (just as there is today – this is written the 1st week of June 2020). The bus driver happened to be a black man and I happen to be a white man. I looked up at him as he blocked my exit; he had tears coming down his cheeks. He spoke to me and said, "You, sir are obviously a Christian." I took his hand in both of my hands and brought it to my mouth and kissed the back of his hand and said to him, "and you, Sir, are obviously my brother!" At that both he and I started crying and you could hear all the air suck out of the bus as I exited, and he and I blew kisses to each other.

These next few stories are scattered around a little as far as the times in my life that they happened. All of a sudden, I remember something that happened forty years ago or 20 or 10 years ago, but I believe they are important, and I will include them as they appear in my mind. Thank you for your patience as you and I go through this process together.

It just occurred to me that as I write these down that I may seem trite or that these events are commonplace and don't affect me much. Nothing could be further from the truth. Each time something happens in my life that I know God's hand was in it somehow is overwhelming to me and leaves me completely undone. At times I don't even know how to thank Him for the generosity of his kindness towards me or the others that have been affected. My heart is consumed with gratitude.

Story #33

Precious to Our Father

One and a half years ago my wife and I went to Maine on vacation to look for her family history there. We had gone into a small coffee shop to get some breakfast. We noticed the young couple they seated at the table next to us seemed a little disturbed. Her face looked as though she had been crying. I leaned over towards them and asked if they were okay. The husband spoke and told us his wife was five and a half months pregnant and they had just come from the doctor who had told them that his wife wouldn't carry this baby to term, and it would be better for her health to terminate the pregnancy now. (They had no children, and this would be their first. They both wanted children and she was heartbroken).

I briefly told them of the woman I had prayed for 30 years prior who had delivered a strong, healthy baby. Then we asked if we could pray for them (when we were all done eating and went outside.) While we were still seated, we exchanged names and phone numbers with them. When we were outside of the coffee shop on the sidewalk, we prayed for them. When we were done praying, the woman spoke up and said they were from Iran and they were Muslims. I told her that the love and kindness of God has no preference of religion, race, color, or sexual orientation. And we would continue to pray until her and her baby were both safe and strong.

Every Friday for the next few months I would text her a prayer. She carried that baby to term and both her and her baby are strong and healthy. She sent me a picture of the baby when they left the hospital. She sent me another picture a year later with her mom and baby, three generations of women in their family. How precious. She also texted me and told me that she is still not sure about Jesus and the whole Christian thing. I told her He is always with her and her daughter and when she needs Him, call His name and He will show up with the same love and kindness and commitment that He did at the beginning. I haven't heard from them since that time months ago. I keep their pictures in my phone, so I remember to pray for them all.

I have learned that this life isn't made up of one event or another. It's a journey and we can help carry others along the path with us (no matter how they come to be a part of our journey). Or we can turn a blind eye and let them fall where they stand. I choose to be one that follows Jesus example (He helped everyone that asked). I am reminded of the woman that came to Him and asked to be healed and He told her "you are not one of mine, should I give the children's' bread to a stranger." She responded, "Yes Master, but even the dog eats the crumbs from the children's table." Then He said, "Go, you are healed." Then Jesus turned to the disciples that were with Him and said to them that the woman that was just healed showed more faith than any of His own people. Jesus Himself praised an outsider because she chose to believe.

Story #34

A Kiss from a Friend

I went to a dear friend's home first thing in the morning. She just lived around the corner from me. I walked there as I had for a couple of weeks. I was doing several projects in her home. We sat on the porch having a cup of coffee and talked about what she wanted to do that day. I was tired and sore and needing some inspiration. We were about to pray as was our practice before work got started when out of nowhere a hummingbird came close to me and was hovering in front of my face. This had happened to me before and I just think they are amazing. Then it came and landed on my wrist. I wear a medical alert bracelet that has a small red emblem on it. The hummingbird sat there for a few seconds pecking at the red medical emblem. Then it flew away. I took that as a sign that God was with me and for me and it just didn't matter how sore or tired I was, He would be there to get me through the day. I was grateful for that moment. It has never happened again, yet I am still grateful and thankful for that moment (my moment) that the King of everything touched me and reminded me that He is with me and for me!!

Story #35

We Can't Out Give Him

This was about 10 years ago. I was preparing to move back to California from Oregon. My health was not good, and I needed to come get treatment, or I probably wouldn't make it. I had given away many tools and jobs that I wasn't going to be able to do. There was a woman that lived a couple miles down the road from me and she bred and raised black labs for service dogs. I stopped there and asked her if she could use a 10'x20' dog run. I had one for my German shepherd to make sure he wouldn't go in the road when I was at work. I recently had to put him down. He was 15 years old and was now deaf and blind. He wouldn't be able to make the journey back to California. She said sure, so I took it apart and took it to her house and unloaded the six panels where she told me to and set it up for her. I had planned to leave the next day. When I was done, she gave me a $100 bill. Up until that time I had been so busy getting everything ready to leave that I hadn't considered that I had no money to pay for the gas to get me there. I thanked her and thanked God for the generosity of His kindness.

I left the next day and started heading south. After a few hours my phone rang, and it was my son. I pulled over to answer it. I was on a small two-lane highway on a mountain pass. My son asked me where I was, and I looked over to the side of the road and the front of my truck was in California and the bed of my truck was in Oregon. I was right at the state line. (My son had encouraged me for a little while to come back to California and get the medical treatment I needed. He is a nurse and a good one). I told him where I was, and he was happy that I had made the commitment to come back to California. Then he told me the reason for his call. (I had been praying with and for him and his wife that she would get pregnant. We had prayed for a couple of years). He had just found out that his wife was pregnant. I sat in the turn out for a few minutes rejoicing with him. That would be my second grandchild. My daughter's son was about 14 months old at that time and when I got to California, I was going to live with them for a bit.

Story #36

He is Ever Watching

I had a friend that was also a contractor and he had bought a home in Lake Tahoe, California. We were both living in Southern California at this time. This was about 15 years ago (there abouts). He and I together were going to add about 2,000 sq. ft. to his existing cabin, which was about 1,200 sq. ft., plus a two-car garage that would be attached to the front corner of the cabin.

I went down one of the ladders to get the nails we needed to attach the rafter hangers to the beams. My friend was prepping the beam on the house when I went down the ladder. He had finished and went over to the garage we had built to cut the end of the beam off (which I did not know.) After I picked up the two boxes of nails, we needed I went to the back of the garage to go back to the ladder. As I stepped through the threshold of the doorway (it was as though someone put both hands on my back and shoved me real hard in the middle of my back between my shoulder blades) I went flying forward about six feet onto my chest. Just as I hit the ground, I heard a deep thud then a whack sound. I looked back and saw a six-foot-long six by 12-inch end cut of a beam leaning against the garage siding. The end of that beam, which weighed about 80 lb., was stuck in the dirt right where I would have been standing had I not been shoved from behind.

My friend looked over the side of the top of the wall where he had just cut the beam (about 30 ft. off the ground). He saw me lying face down on the ground and yelled my name with concern in his voice. I yelled back (I'm okay, I'll be right up). When I got up on the floor of the second story, he had come over to the top of the ladder. I told him what had happened and that the cut off beam would have landed on my head had God not done something. At the same time, we both said, "Thank you Jesus!!"

Now it may not have killed me or left me with permanent brain damage (although most likely it would have), God in His mercy, kindness, and compassion acted on my behalf to save me. No prayer was offered and I didn't even know I was in danger. And my thanks are all He gets for all He does. And that is all He requires. He tells us we are to have thankful, grateful hearts, "For ALL HIS benefits".

Story #37

Even Underground

This story and the next one were both about 43 years ago. I was in my early 20's and about to have my first child be born in a few weeks. I was working with my dad doing underground construction. We were tunneling under a concrete sidewalk to make a tie in of four-inch pipe to pull telephone cable into a manhole which was in the street behind where we were digging. I had broken through to the trench line from the pothole I had dug. I had gotten down into the hold and had begun to clean out the tunnel. I was lying on my belly with a shovel in my hands getting the dirt level so we could push the four-foot pipe through. I was about five feet deep below ground level. I only had a couple more shovelfuls to go and we could push the four-inch pipe through into the pothole next to the curb of the street. When the sidewalk broke off and caved in on me covering my head and body in dirt with a 300 lb. piece of concrete on top of the dirt covering me.

My dad and my co-worker were standing on the ground above me when it happened. (About six feet away). My dad jumped into the trench digging with his hands trying to find and uncover my face. My co-worker grabbed a 90 lb. breaker that was nearby and fired up the compressor. He began trying to break the piece of concrete on top of me with the breaker. (So, the pieces were lighter so they could be lifted out of the hole the cave in created.) My dad and my co-worker both finished about the same time. I had been buried there about four and a half minutes. I had dirt packed in my eyes, ears, and nose. It took another couple of minutes to finish digging out the rest of my body. They had me lay on the ground and poured water all over my head and face to get the dirt off of me and out of my nose, ears and eyes (I didn't have any in my mouth.) That is probably what kept me alive. I had not tried to breathe. I later found out that had I tried to breathe through my mouth, I would have suffocated. God was able to keep me alive for four and a half minutes under the ground without any air. It was a miracle. Not the first in my life nor would it be the last. So grateful for the love, grace, and kindness of my great and mighty King who never leaves any of us nor forsakes any of us. Thank you, Jesus!

Story #38

Willing to Trust

When my son was 18 months old, his platelet count dropped to almost nothing. The doctors began doing all kinds of tests. At first, they told us that they thought he had Leukemia. Then later told us he had severe food allergies, so he was taken off all foods. (The only thing he ate for months was raw goat's milk and raw goat milk cheese. Then every few weeks they would add one more non allergenic food at a time. Nothing was helping much. This went on a little over three years, testing his blood constantly.

When he was four years old, I took him in for another bout of blood work. As the nurse came close to him as he sat in the chair, he stuck his arm out as he had done so many times before. She took his hand and wrapped the rubber tube around his upper arm and took the needle in her hand and stuck it into his vein. My son didn't blink, flinch, or even take a deep breath. He just sat there smiling at the nurse. Watching this left me undone. This small child had experienced so much pain in his little life that the sharp burning pain of the needle going into his precious little body had no effect on him whatsoever. The thought of this caused me to start crying. My son at four years old reached out his other hand and took my hand in his. (He was reaching out to comfort me!) Such courage, grace, and peace coming from him towards me.

God spoke to my heart at that moment and told me that if I would just trust Him as my son does, He would take care of this. I cried out to Him in my heart (right there) that I was willing to trust, but He would have to work it into me. The results from those tests were a lot better and over the next year his blood was changed, and his platelets were in the normal range. And they have stayed there ever since. I don't even remember what the final diagnosis was. My son will be 43 years old next month. He is six feet, three inches tall and has been a nurse for 20 years. He still is a peaceful, gentle, compassionate person. I still learn from his example.

Story #39

Give It to God

Over the years, myself and sometimes with others, have had the opportunity to pray with couples that had problems with infertility. Many had prayed for years and had gone through all kinds of treatment regiments with no avail. On six different occasions, after praying with and for these couples, over a period of time all six of these couples conceived and gave birth to wonderful, beautiful, healthy babies. I still see some of these people. Some of those babies are grown now and have babies of their own.

"We have a good, good Father! Full of mercy and compassion."

Story #40

How my wife and I became a couple!!

I came back to California from Oregon 10 years ago. I went through a lot of medical things the first year. When those were over, I went back to the church I had been involved with 25 years prior.

I got involved with some of our outreach endeavors. One of the men I was working with invited me to a home group. I started going once a week for a couple of months. I didn't really know anyone very well. The man that I served with that had invited me to the home group asked if I could help that Saturday to help one of the home group member's move, and I said I would be happy to. That Saturday several of the men in the group and myself moved a single mom and her adult son from one location to another about eight miles away. I had seen this woman before. She was the secretary of the home group and stood up and gave the announcements at the start of the meetings. I had seen her before I had started attending the home group. The first Sunday morning that I came back to the church after being gone for 20 years, I was kind of wandering around just looking at everything; the church had moved into a new facility and it was very different.

I went up the stairs and stood at the rail looking down at the area by the front door. There was a booth where people come and check their kids in for Sunday School. As I looked at the people behind the booth, there was one person that stood out. From my position upstairs I could see the love and Spirit of God resting on this woman there. She was speaking to the children and parents in such a way that the love of Jesus was embracing them, as they entered the door for Sunday School full of joy. This single mom we had just moved was that woman so full of the love and Spirit of Jesus. (She treated all of us moving her that day with the same kindness and joy as I saw when she received the children at church.)

A couple of months later I was invited to her home with several others for a Christmas dinner. I came and enjoyed the evening. At that time, she offered all of us to come with her to go to the Rose

Parade Floats the day before the parade. Some of her family members drove the floats and could get us in to see them. There were four of us that went that day. It was fun and beautiful; we spent a few hours there looking at all the flowers and designs (I was the only man that had accepted the invitation that day). In the car on the drive home God began to speak to my heart concerning this woman that had recently come into my life. (I wouldn't even say we were friends – we had only spent a few hours of time over the past several months in each other's presence). God asked me if I would be willing to see her socially. I replied in my heart and head (not out loud as I was sitting in a car with three others and the woman, I am talking about was driving the car) NO!! I am not interested in seeing anyone socially. About 10 minutes later God asked me the same question. Would you be interested in seeing her socially? My answer was the same, "NO! I really don't want to. I want to invest whatever time I have left into my family." Another 10 minutes went by and God touched my heart again with the same question. "Would you be interested in seeing her socially?"

This time instead of answering with a no I asked a question of Him. Father is that something you want. Do you want me to see her socially? His answer back was, "Yes! That would please Me!" So I began to pray that God would confirm this in her heart. I wasn't going to speak of this or encourage it in any way. If this is what you want for both of us, You Lord, cause it to happen.

At that moment we got to my house. I was the first one out of the car. I thanked them all for a lovely time and told them I would see them at the group meeting coming up the next week. I went into my apartment confused but content. If that was God speaking to me (and I was certain it was, I had heard His voice and let Him lead me through most of my life for over 40 years at that time) I went in and laid down and put on one of my favorite worship CD's. Before it was over my phone went off letting me know there was a text. The text came from the woman who had been my hostess for the past two days. The woman that my God had just told me that He would take pleasure in me cultivating a more intimate relationship with. That text was the longest text I have ever received before or since.

Earlier that the day, I kept calling her sister. She wrote that she felt uncomfortable with that and she didn't know why but that she "did not want to be my sister." I text her back and told her God was speaking to me about that in the car on the way home and that we really should talk about it in person. (It was not something I wanted to try to explain to her on the phone.) So, we agreed to meet at the park down the street from my apartment when she got off work the next day. I told her all that God had spoken to me and also the answers I had given Him.

I was scheduled for surgery a hernia surgery a few weeks later. We talked on the phone each day after she got home from work. The day of my surgery she picked me up from the hospital and took me home. A few days after we went to night church, it was after service I'd realized something wasn't quite right and asked her to take me back to the hospital. As soon as they did an initial examination, they scheduled me for emergency surgery. They found when they had done the hernia surgery, they had accidentally nicked my bowel and it had been leaking into my belly causing a massive infection. The following day she came back to pick me up to take me back home. As we were going over what was going to take place for the next six days, that I had to basically reopen the wound by removing and repacking the wound and pour in antibiotics. I shared with her all would be fine even though I live alone I'll I be fine. I can tear the wound open and do this. She said, "No! You come to our place with me and my son, and when I get home from work, I will do what needs to be done. Please." As she was adamant, I agreed to come to their home. That first day when she came home from work, we laid a towel down on the hall bath floor and I took my shirt off and the bandages off. Just as she started opening the wound her son came in the front door. She poured the saline to clean out the wound and then put the antibiotics into the wound, which at that moment my whole body flexed in pain as the solution burned into the wound. He yelled at her, "What are you doing?" She explained that I had an infection and that I would be there with them for a few days and that every day for a few days she would be doing this when she gets home from work.

We were married eight months later. We have been married now for eight years and in that time; I have had over 20 more surgeries. I don't know what I would have done had she not heard God speaking to her heart concerning me. We have both had many opportunities to stand up and with and for each other over these years. We both need each other and are blessed and at peace knowing that what we sow into each other completes each of us. So grateful to my sweet Jesus that He knew I needed this lovely, godly, precious woman in my life to move forward with all that He had planned for both of us. I know I have at least one more surgery left to go. And we will take that as it comes just as we have done with all the rest. In fact, this next story is about the last surgery I had.

Story #41

(A little over 2 years ago)

I had lived in and with cruel and brutal pain for a few years. I was taking three morphine tabs a day just to be able to stand and walk. My spine was in terrible condition, five of my disks were gone. They had been destroyed from a lifetime of abusing my body with the types of work that I did. Three of my nerves were caught in my spine when it fused itself together because of the absence of the discs.

I scheduled surgery for my spine. The thin bone on five of my vertebrae had to be cut off and the three nerves that were being pinched had to be relocated. The surgery was going to take about seven hours.

On the day of the surgery, the surgeon stood in front of me and told me I had a 50/50 chance of surviving the surgery. Because I had already had so many surgeries when they went to wake me up from the surgery I may not wake up. If I woke up, I would no longer have the pain in my back (which shot up to my head and down to my feet). However, I would probably never be able to walk again. I smiled at him and said, "My God is just way bigger than that." He said, "I am not really a person of faith, so I don't really know anything about that." I said, "I am not expecting a miracle from you, but I am expecting a miracle from my God. You just have to do your part – I don't want to hear or see an oops on the video." He said, "Good enough." While in surgery, my wife, and a sister from church were there praying for me. I knew that all of my family and friends were praying, as well as many others that had been added to our prayer chain and asked to pray.

I didn't wake up until the following morning. When I woke up, the brutal unrelenting pain that I had lived with for years was gone. It had been the first thing I felt when I opened my eyes each morning for years. I heard God's voice telling me, "Get up!" I didn't even know if my legs would work at this time. So I tried to wiggle my toes and I could. Then I bent my legs and brought my feet up towards my body and they moved. Then I threw the blanket off of me and slid off the bed and grabbed hold of the two I.V. poles that were hooked up to me and walked to the nurse's station and told them I wanted to go home. They said, "Are you crazy, get back in bed." One of them escorted me back to my bed. The surgeon came in about an hour later. He asked, "What's going on? I heard you were up walking." I told him God had told me to get up, so I did. I then told him, "I'd like to go home." He then told me, "I was a pain in the ass! There is nothing I did that would allow you to walk; now I have to write this up to the AMA as a miracle." Then he said, "I am still not a person of faith. But you tell your crew they can be part of my team anytime." They did a bunch of tests and told me I could go home that evening after they finished all their tests. I called my wife and told her I could walk, and she could pick me up on her way home from work.

The surgeon came in later that day and told me that "I will always be frail and fragile and that I needed to respect that. And and not try to lift over 20 lb." That if I start to feel pain, for me to get down and stay down for a while.

This surgery was done two and a half years ago, and I still get up and walk every day. I can't bend over much or very well. When I want to do something that requires me to bend, I get down on my knees or even lay on the ground to do what it is I want to do. I even have had to put myself in a bed a few times from making poor choices and trying to do more than my body is willing or able to do. However, I have not had to take a pain pill in the two and a half years since my surgery. So grateful and thankful for the generosity of God's kindness and faithfulness towards me. Showing up to do for me what I could not do for myself.

Story #42

Even in the Womb, He is There

My wife and I have the joy and blessing of sharing five grandchildren, the youngest of these being about 14 months now. About a year earlier, when she was still in the womb, we found out that she had a rare genetic condition known as OI (Osteogenesis Imperfecta or aka Brittle Bone Disease). After running many tests, we were told they found that she had already had seven fractures in her tiny little body.

We put her on every prayer list that we knew of. There were hundreds of people praying for her in her last two months in the womb. When she was born, they retested her and found that all seven of the earlier fractures had already healed.

She weighed nearly 7 lbs. when she was born. Generally, most babies lose a little weight when after going home. Yet she not only lost weight, but then continued to not gain weight. 5 days after birth she got down to under 6 lbs. She spent her first two and a half months in the NICU trying to figure out how to help her thrive. What was so amazing to us all was how very tiny, young and yet very alert and aware of us all she was at this very young age. She was a joy and a delight.

Finally, at the end of those two and half months, lots of prayer and the help of many doctors and nurses she made it to nine pounds. She was finally able to eat, keep it down and gain weight! She'd made it to the weight marker they set, before she'd be allowed to go home.

She is ten months old now and is up to over 13 lbs. She will probably always be tiny and may possibly need surgery to help her be able to stand and walk. She has had a few bone fractures in her first 10 months. However, our God has been so faithful and compassionate towards her each time. One her last fractures was re-x-rayed after it occurred to figure out a treatment plan. Yet within those three days after that fracture, it had healed and no treatment was required.

We have a good, good Father and if we will ask for His help based only on our need of Him, He will show up in many and different ways. Either personally or by Him sending one of His angels. Yes, angels. They are real, they are here walking among us to bring hope, help, power, and encouragement as we walk out this journey. This I know for sure!!

"In Conclusion"

He is the God of All Hope

If you can only remember two things from these stories remember these two. When you are crying out to Jesus for yourself or someone else, pay no attention to the voices of those around you. They may not need from Jesus what you need from Him!

As the blind man cried out to Jesus for mercy, the crowd around him was uncomfortable and even embarrassed and began to tell the man to "be quiet. Leave the teacher alone." (As though his cries were unacceptable). The man cried out even louder, "Jesus, Son of David, have mercy on me." You see after that gathering was over, those people shushing that man were going home to see their children. However, the blind man knew that "at that very moment in time might be the only chance he ever had to see his children." So, when those around you don't have the same need as you, ignore them and cry out even louder (whether it is for you or someone else.) With even more intensity and desperation in your voice, "cry out."

For I have learned that it is the willful, deliberate expression to my God of my desperate need of Him that moves His heart and hands to answer the request I make. Whether they are for me or for someone else, those around you or me may never understand the desperation of the need we have and our willingness to lay it down at the feet and mercy of our Sweet Jesus.

The second thing I hope you remember is this, I know He found me, I know He saved me, I know He loves me. There is a verse in the Bible that declares, "He sought me out and found me, and it is with His deep abiding love for me that He draws me to Himself." I know from personal experience that truth applies to ALL people.

I am not willing to wait for heaven. When the King of the Glory of Heaven lives in me, and because He has been so committed to so generously pour out His love, kindness, forgiveness, mercy, and compassion on me, His fire burns in my belly. The flames of His love consume my heart. I want to give to anyone in need the same gifts of His presence that He has chosen to invest in me. There are many better men and women than I could ever hope to be. However, my hope is based on nothing more than my desperate NEED of Him. "To be fully known and fully loved in spite of myself is humbling and empowering at the same moment in time. For at the end of the day, I have nothing to lose." I have no fear, for "He, the King of everything, is with me and for me!!

As I consider all that has been said of my God and all His host of angels that come with Him, I would be remiss, even unkind or cruel if I didn't give you, the reader, an opportunity to know Him personally and intimately. If you don't know this God in all His splendor and glory, you can!!

There is a verse in the Bible that says, "Whoever is willing is invited to come." So if you are one of those that are "willing" to meet Him and know Him as your loving Father, and faithful friend, and invite the fullness of His love, kindness, compassion, grace, and mercy to come to you by His powerful Holy Spirit, PLEASE take just a moment and pray the prayer that is here on this page, and your life and your thinking will never be the same. You will never again be alone or hopeless. For He is the "God of all hope."

Prayer

"O Father in heaven, great King of everything. Come to me now in this very moment. I have found that within myself I do not have what I need to be self-sufficient and stand alone in this world. I am in need of you to clean my heart and mind and make them whole. Forgive me where I have fallen short of being that person that I know you want me to be. I give you now permission to change my thoughts, words, actions, hopes, and dreams so I can live in peace with You and others. I am Yours now and You are mine. Thank you for your mercy, and for hearing this prayer! Amen.